Million Dollar Ecommerce

A Beginner's Guide to Building
an Unforgettable Ecommerce Brand.
Pick a Profitable Idea, Start a New Online Business
and Scale It to a 7-Figure Income Source.

Red Mikhail

OTHER FBA BOOKS

AMAZON FBA Step by Step (by Red Mikhail)_– to help you get started with Amazon FBA (the basics)

FBA Product Research 101 – an in depth guide to product research

Amazon Keyword Research 101 – an in depth guide to Amazon keyword research

FBA Product Sourcing Blueprint – a step by step blueprint on sourcing products and shipping it to Amazon/your preferred destination

Amazon FBA Sales Boost – 33 little tricks to triple your Amazon sales

These are also available as audiobooks.

You can find the whole series here:

https://www.amazon.com/gp/product/B086QZCJQQ

TABLE OF CONTENTS

Preface

Que Trailer... Insert *Honest Trailer from YouTube voice guy here.*

From the author that brought you the instant classic and the single most reviewed FBA book of all-time, Amazon FBA for Beginners, comes a new adventure that will take you through the process of creating a million-dollar brand. This is MILLION DOLLAR ECOMMERCE: A Beginner's Guide to Building an Unforgettable Ecommerce Brand.

Alright, sorry – I got carried away, enough of the hype.

Hey there, Red here and this is part 6 of the Amazon FBA series. Technically, this book isn't really solely about FBA or Amazon. It's about creating a successful ecommerce business from idea to execution by creating your own brand. The reason I'm putting it as part of the FBA series are 2 folds:

1 – This will reach more people interested in starting an ecommerce business. Since this series is getting hundreds of readers every day, it is likely that this will get some attention as well.

2 – I still recommend that most beginner ecommerce business owners (whether they create their own brand

or start with arbitrage) still sell their products first on Amazon.

And as always, the value of my books isn't really in the number of pages that it has. For me, it will always be about the actionable stuff. The truth is, I have no idea if this book will be 50 pages or 100 pages. Obviously, I have some sort of outline and estimate but I only use those as a guide and not as a "number of pages" goal. If you're the type of person whose focus is action and not just information, then I'm pretty confident that you'll love this one.
In addition, expect it to be super casual. This is just me talking to you in my living room, drinking beers, and just having a good time.

FOR BEGINNERS ONLY?

Although there will be some advance tactics and foundational stuff that ALL ecommerce business owners should learn, my primary target for this book is the beginner market.

If you're someone who already has a product line and someone who's already selling online for 3 years or more, then this book is not for you.

I try to cater to everybody and give as much info as I can but this book would serve you best if you're someone who's just getting started.

Introduction

If you think that it's too late now to start an e-commerce business, then you are greatly mistaken. The ecommerce industry is still growing and it will continue to grow for the years to come. This is probably one of the biggest (if not the biggest) opportunity of our lifetime. Millions of people will put (and are putting) themselves into a much better financial situation because of ecommerce. If you're reading this book and you're committed to taking action, then I see no reason why you won't be part of that movement.

Here are the best reasons why you should start an ecommerce business today:

#1 – It's Growing at a Break Neck Speed

It's crazy fast how ecommerce is growing. By starting your own business, you'll be able to ride the trend and you'll be able to build and grow a business faster than most people could ever imagined. And since *ecom* is a global business, you basically have the whole world as your potential market!

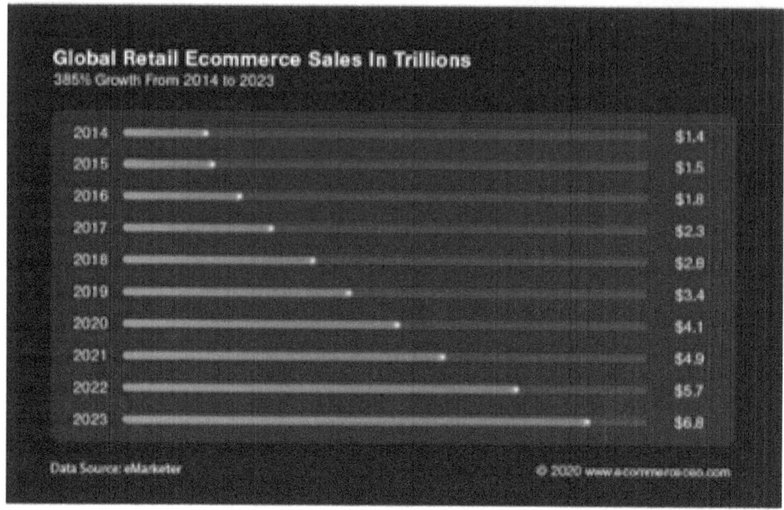

[Image 0.1]

#2 – Lots of New Niches to Target

There are literally hundreds if not thousands of potential niche markets to target. You don't have to rely on the niches that did well a few years ago. Today, you can make 7 figures even on niches that most people never heard of. There are new niches and new opportunities popping up every single day and you could be the one dominating that market.

The key is to create a product line that a market segment will buy over and over again.

#3 – Freedom Lifestyle

Because there's so much money to be made from ecommerce, it can help you live a financially comfortable life without sacrificing the things that you value most. The truth is, you can design your business in whatever size you like it to be. If you want to make 200k per year after tax and work 4 hours per day, then you can definitely do that. If you're more of a pure-bred entrepreneur and you enjoy the process of running a business, then you can spend as much time on your business as you want. One doesn't have to be better than the other. The point is you have a choice and building and running your own ecommerce brand allows you to have that choice.

1,000 FT. OVERVIEW

Allow me to give you an overview of how this whole ecommerce brand building process works.

Let me break it down chapter by chapter.

In **Chapter 1 – How to Create a Million Dollar Brand: Differentiate**, I will show you why you need to build your own brand and how to actually differentiate yourself from other sellers out there. You'll learn 4 different effective strategies on how you can stand out from the crowd and how to implement these to your own business. After this chapter, you'll see how big the opportunity is and you'll have a better understanding of the concept of branding and how it works in the ecommerce world.

In **Chapter 2 - How to Find Your Idea**, I'll show you how to find your niche or idea and then I'll show you how to come up with products that are more likely to have a demand and ready buyers at your fingertips. In this chapter, you'll learn how to rely less on tools and rely more on your "problem solving" skills to find the perfect idea for your new ecommerce business.

In **Chapter 3 - Product Sourcing Made Simple**, I will teach you exactly how to research potential manufacturers, evaluate suppliers, and source your products the right way. This is where most people get stuck, understandably, because this is the part where you invest money in the business. If you can get pass this part, then you'll already be head & shoulders against most people trying to start their own ecom brand.

In **Chapter 4 - How to Sell Your Physical Products**, I will teach you where and how to actually sell the products you sourced/created. I'll discuss the platforms you can use (i.e. Amazon/Shopify), the advantages and disadvantages of those platforms, and the best ways to drive traffic to your online store - both free and paid.

In **Chapter 5 - How to Scale Your Ecommerce Brand**, we'll discuss how to take your business to the next level. You'll learn the top 5 strategies most successful ecommerce brands do so you can create a 7-figure per year business. You'll learn stuff like *cart abandonment, AOV, time sensitive deals, upsells*, ads scaling, and other ecommerce strategies. By the end of this chapter, you'll have a buffet of actionable brand building and sales-getting strategies for you to build a 7-figure ecommerce brand.

THE REALISTIC MATH BEHIND A 7-FIGURE BUSINESS

Before you move on to chapter 1, I want to give you a *paint by the numbers* look at how you can create a 7-figure ecommerce brand.

If you're just starting out, it is very unlikely that your first and only product will make 7 figures per year. It can happen for sure, but that's just not a realistic expectation to set for yourself. Instead, I want you to focus on creating a product line up that complements each other. We will discuss more on this later but for now, let's focus on the numbers.

Let's say that the average price of the products you sell is $35. **If you want to gross 7 figures per year, then you have to sell at least 4 different products at $35 each and sell 20 pieces per product per day.**

Here's the math breakdown:

4 [Products] x 20 [Pieces Per Day] = 80 [Pieces Sold Per Day Sold]

80 [Pieces Per Day Sold] x $35 [Price in USD] = $2,800 Per Day

2,800 Per Day x 30 [Days] = $84,000 Per Month

$84,000 Per Month is basically 7-Figures Per Year

Now you might be thinking, damn, I can never sell 80 pieces of anything per day! That's too hard. Well, it is but it's not impossible. Remember, Amazon alone gets millions and millions of visitors per day and customers are buying billions worth of products per year. If you think about it hard enough, you'll see that selling 80 pieces per day of your products is a very realistic goal. Heck, you can do that just by selling on Amazon alone.

Imagine what would happen if you expand to creating your own store and actively advertise/market your own products? I'm telling you, it can get crazy awesome!

By looking at this simplified version of our business model, you'll now have a clearer understanding of how you can make this business work for you. Look at our sample numbers again, that number is possible for anyone and that someone could be you.

Let's do this!

Chapter 1
How to Create a Million Dollar Brand: Differentiate

First of all, let's define what a brand is and what it isn't. A brand is basically a business with the ability to roll out multiple products and make those products as successful if not more successful than the first one. A brand is an entity that separates you from the other "me too" products out there. What a brand isn't are logos, brand names, name in the building, or company videos - those are just part of the brand and they aren't the brand itself.

Why You Need to Be Different

There's a lot of good products out there and you need to stand out if you want to stay in business and thrive. **BEING DIFFERENT** is crucial because it allows you to say "Hey, I'm here – notice me!" without acting like a needy stalker. Having a brand automatically puts you in the category of the cool kids who gets noticed by almost everybody. Grateful Dead (the band) is still thriving today not because they're trying to be the best band ever. They don't care about that. By now, they already have an identity and a solid fan base whom they care about serving. Right now, they're just trying to be the best version of themselves. They're just trying to be the best version of who they already are. That doesn't mean they aren't evolving. I mean, for god's sake they hired John Mayer (a pop star! A far cry from their original front man Jerry Garcia) as their newest member since 2015. But the fan base accepted Mayer because, a.) he's actually really good in playing with the band **(in terms of ecommerce, he is a good complementary product),** and b.) he isn't the main attraction of the Grateful Dead, Mayer is only part of the bigger picture.

Whether you know the band or not, I do hope that you got the point I'm trying to say. It's not about being the best. It's not about not having any identity and being boring. It's not about being stale and never taking any risks. It's about being different and trying to evolve by giving the customers what they want and need.

So, with all these talk about differentiation, how do you actually do it? What are the practices that you can apply so you can differentiate your brand from the millions of products and businesses out there?

There are 4 MAIN WAYS I subscribe to when it comes to brand differentiation. Each of them is important and I make sure that I always apply ALL of them for my ecommerce brands.

THE CORE FOUR OF BRAND DIFFERENTIATION

#1 - Product Differentiation
#2 - Brand Look & Feel Differentiation
#3 - Marketing & Positioning Differentiation
#4 - Customer Service & Customer Experience
Differentiation

I'm sure there are other ways to differentiate but these are the core 4 that I follow. Feel free to research more on this if you want to. I do believe that these are enough for you to build a 7-figure ecommerce brand.

How to Build an Ecommerce Brand – Differentiation Strategies

#1 - Product Differentiation

This is bar none, the most important differentiation strategy of all. I would even claim that the other 3 doesn't work as well if you do not implement this one. I repeat: this is the most important way of building an ecom brand. Highlight that, write it down, put it on a note, and attach it to your fridge! By having a product that is actually different from the others, it will be much easier to build a business that will thrive in good times and in bad times. You can be different **by actually being different** - I know - what a concept, right? (LOL).

The key factor to remember when it comes to product differentiation is this: WHAT DO YOUR CUSTOMERS WANT AND NEED.

What They Want:

If you listen to your customers and you did your product research the right way, then you'll know exactly what they want when it comes to the product you are offering. For example, there's a segment of the "whey protein" buyers who doesn't like any sugar with what they're drinking. What can you do to solve this problem? What are the potential solutions for this issue? Well, you can put less sugar on your product. That's the most basic solution. But to make your offer more compelling, you can come up with possible substitute to sugar and put it on your whey protein brand instead. You can substitute sugar with neotame, aspartame, stevia or monk fruit. These are "artificial sweeteners" (but natural sugars) derived from extraction from various sources. Obviously, you still have to weigh the pros and cons before you put any of that stuff to your product. In this case, you're serving the market by removing what they want to be removed and adding a better substitute at the same time.

What They Need:

To serve the customers through your product, you also have to give them what they need. Sometimes, they don't even know what they need until you present it to them.

The most common customer needs are the following:

1 – Fair Price. All customers want a fair price for what they are buying. Don't get too greedy when it comes to profit and always offer fair market value for your products.

2 – Functionality. This is an obvious one. Your product has to be functional and it must be able to do what it promises to do.

3 – Effective/Efficient. Customers want a product that can give them the best and fastest result at the same time. *I.e. If you're selling a butcher knife, you better be damn sure that it can do its job fast and efficient. That means cutting should feel almost effortless.*

4 – Transparency. Make sure that you always mention the materials and ingredients your products are made of. This is especially true in consumable products, but important for any items nonetheless.

5 – Accessibility. Is your product available and easy to buy? You can put your products either on Amazon and your own website (or both).

6 – Options. Customers also need different options. Those options can either be about sizes, colors, types of ingredient, materials used, etc.

Note: In the next chapter, we will have a section called "How to Make Your Product Different" and we'll dive deep on the exact strategies to follow for product differentiation. I'll also give more examples so you'll have a clearer understanding of how this all works.

#2 - Brand Look & Feel Differentiation

This is what most people think about when they hear the word "brand." But as I've already told you, this is only part of the whole thing.
It is important to nail this one right at the very beginning since the way your brand's *look and feel* is going to be the foundation of how people perceived your brand.

Note: *This is especially true if you're selling outside Amazon.*

Here are the top 3 things to look at when it comes to your brand's look and feel.

#1 - Logo

Your logo is a combination of text and imagery. It acts as a visual representation of your company. It's the thing that represents your company virtually speaking. Since they can't see you (the founder) or any of your potential employees, your logo can act as the representative of your company. The logo also separates your brand to other peoples' brand in your niche.

Look at what your competitors' logo look like and try to be as different as possible.

Here are some of the best practices to remember when it comes to creating your logo:

- The color affects how people perceived your brand.
- Don't make the text too long.
- Have something easy to remember.
- Make the text as readable as possible.
- It should look timeless.
- Use less than 3 colors combined,
- Don't use any complicated new colors, just use any of the ones from the rainbow.
- Make sure that it'll work for variety of industries.

- Ensure that it looks good on black & white background which is going to be where most people will see your logo.
- Look at the logos of your competitors and try to be as different as possible (color and font text are great differentiators).

If you're just getting started, I recommend that you start with Fiverr for cheap logos but hire someone better as soon as you get your first few sales. *Re-invest your profits in your business and years from now, you'll be glad that you did that.*

#2 - Colors (Palettes)

Another factor that affects your brand's perceived value are the colors that you use in pretty much everything your company owns. You can use your choice of colors not only in your product/packages but also in your marketing materials, website, social media content, etc.

According to a few studies, the color affects more than 60% of buying decisions made by customers. Colors basically affect how they perceive your brand as a whole.

For example, blue emits tranquility, security, loyalty and trust. But it also emits coldness, fear, and masculinity. Yellow says bright, sunny, and energetic, but it also says unstable and irresponsible. There's no perfect color and it's not the only factor to look at for your ecommerce business, but it's an important one nonetheless.

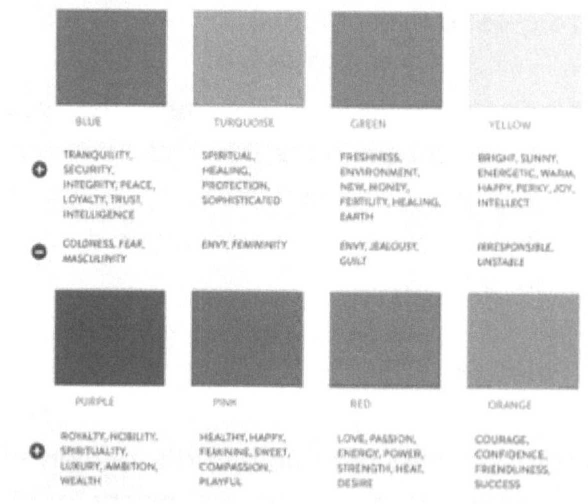

[Image 1.1]

Source: quicksrpout.com

HOW TO CHOOSE A CORE COLOR

It's honestly pretty simple: **"Know Your Target Demographic"**

Before you choose your top 2 to 3 dominating colors for your brand, the core colors you can use for your social media, websites, products, etc., make sure that you know WHO your customers are. *Are they mostly single people? Are they men or women? How old or how young are them?*

You need to choose your colors based on what they value or who they identify with.

If I'm selling to primarily men, then I'll probably choose between blue, red , black, and white (very neutral color).

If I'm selling to women (say beauty products), I'll most likely choose light pink, green, orange, or white.

These all depends as well on the product you are selling. But it has to match the energy that you want your product to emanate.

Quicksprout has a very detailed article about this and I recommend that you check it out here:

https://www.quicksprout.com/the-right-ecommerce-color-schemes/

#3 - Fonts

Honestly, I wouldn't worry about this too much in the beginning. The key is to start with safe and proven fonts to use.

Here are some fonts to choose for your ecommerce business and the corresponding niches that matches their perceived energy:

Montserrat (more industrial – electronic & industrial parts)

Crimson Text (skincare, yoga, spa, and other lifestyle products)

Oswald (for fitness, technology industry)

Overlock (for a little more playful look, clothes, baby products, and products serving the feminine side of things)

Playfair Display (dresses, beauty products, also feminine feel)

Remember to use the font of your choice in all your company assets. (advertising materials, marketing materials, website, sales pages, social media posts).

#3 - Marketing & Positioning Differentiation

People hate boring brands. Boring brands are dying and no one wants to be associated with them.

So how do we create a brand that's exciting and a brand that people love to talk about? How do we create what they call a "brand voice?" *Something that resonates with your target market and something that has a personality…*

Step 1 – Know who you're talking to

The first step is to know exactly who your target market is.

Here are some useful things to know about your target market:
A – Age Range
B – Gender
C – Nationality
D – Possible Political Leaning (Right, Left, Center)
E – Their Insecurities, Their Goals, What Product Similar to Yours They Are Currently Buying and What They Hate About These Products
(you'll learn how to research this in chapter 2)

Step 2 – Define who you want to be

Define who you are as a company. Are you fun and quirky? Are you serious and corporate like? I wouldn't say one is better than the other. But have some personality and let that personality define your business. In addition, that brand personality should match your audience. If you have younger buyers, then it makes sense to be a little playful with the language and tone you're using as a brand. If you have an older audience, then it's alright to be a little serious and straightforward.

At the same time, you have to know who you want to be as a brand.

Who are you as a company? What is your personality?

PERSONAL TO BUSINESS SPECTRUM

How personal do you want to be? How casual do you want to be perceived at?

I.e. Ryan Reynold's Gin Aviation.

Self-deprecating, funny, slightly laid back, feel good and feel awesome type of brand.

You can tell by their commercials that they appeal to a younger audience who doesn't like to take themselves seriously. And when I say younger, I say between 25-40.

Not all of us have the charisma of Ryan Reynolds and we don't necessarily have to have that anyway. We can still build a personality for our brand no matter who we are. We just have to commit to a certain attitude and know what we stand for as a company. Those Ryan Reynold Gin Aviation commercials work not because Ryan Reynolds is a big celebrity. It works because we know that Ryan Reynold is being an authentic (funny, charismatic, laid back) version of himself on those commercials – which is what we already know him for even before Aviation Gin.

EASY LANGUAGE TO INSIDER LANGUAGE SPECTRUM

Another thing to consider is the type of language you are using.

This will again all depend on your target market. How sophisticated are your buyers? Are you targeting the ones who are already in this market for a long-time? Or are you trying to convert new ones to join your market?

Here's an example I got from digitalmarketer.com (so credit to those guys!).

Bulletproof sells food and supplements for people looking to improve their health and lifestyles. Their founder Dave Asprey is well-versed in biohacking jargon—but you don't see a word of jargon in the emails to their subscribers.

Why? Because their customer avatar isn't an expert in the health space; they're an average person trying to figure out how to live a better lifestyle. That's why you'll see an easy language brand voice in Bulletproof's emails to their subscribers where they explain what refined carbohydrates are and why they're bad for you in easy-to-read language:

[Image 1.2]

Bulletproof doesn't use (or barely use) any of the insider language that "veterans" in this market use. They want to convert new people in their market so they have to use easy to understand language in their emails, website, and market materials so people would understand what they're trying to say.

How about your brand? Where does your business lie in the easy language to insider language spectrum? Only you can answer that.

#4 - Customer Service & Customer Experience Differentiation

CUSTOMER SERVICE

Nowadays, customer service is one of the main keys to long-term brand trust. Ironically, a lot of ecommerce brands today have terrible customer service so it won't be that hard to differentiate. By investing in customer service, you'll be above and beyond what customers expect. I dare you to call most of the companies you are patronizing right now, you'll probably go straight to a machine telling you how "you are important to us" while they make you wait for 2 hours only to be served by someone who can barely understand what you're saying. That's the kind of customer service that we're expecting nowadays. Our expectations are so low that we're not even expecting a reply on most of our customer service emails. All of these low expectation talk reminds me of this meme:

[Image 1.3]

Anyway, it's easy to solve this problem.

Invest in your customer service. There should be someone manning the emails from customers 24/7.

Yes, 24/7.

I know that this may eat up a bit of your profits in the beginning, but trust me, this is something that you have to do to build a brand that people love and trust.

Start with that then expand to having a phone number for customers to call. For now, a 24/7 customer email support is enough especially if you're just getting started.

CUSTOMER EXPERIENCE

There's a lot of ways to differentiate with customer experience. Here are the best ones I apply in all of my brands:

Easy Navigation – Your website should be clean and easy to navigate. Make your products easy to find in your website. In addition, they should be able to easily find customer support if they need it.

Packaging – People love a good unboxing experience. You can differentiate by having a premium feel for your products and making the box/packaging as appealing as possible. (i.e. Apple products)

Build Great Product Pages – Create product pages that are sleek and clean looking. It should show the product images, a few benefits of the product, and then a big add to cart/buy button.

Checkout Process – It bugs me that to this day, a lot of ecommerce stores I see are still using clunky and outdated checkout process. If I'm the customer, I should be able to know exactly what items I bought, how many I bought, and where to put my payment details. In addition, I should be able to look at the checkout process and trust that I'm not getting scammed. Add some trust badges on the page where they have to put their payment information.

Email Onboarding – Make your customers feel welcomed when they buy your product/s. Always send an order confirmation that shows the summary of their order plus the expected date of when it will arrive on their doorstep. In addition, try to be a little personal by adding some kind of thank you message or any informative message as well. For example, in your thank you email, you can send them additional information and link them to a blog (preferably your blog) about how to maximize what they just bought from your store. This adds value and shows that you care about your customers.

Faster Shipping and Easy Tracking – People are impatient nowadays. We just want to get what we ordered as fast as possible. Also, we want access to our order via easy tracking. If you can provide these 2, then you'll already be head & shoulders above your competition.

Optimize for Mobile – Make your website optimized for mobile. More than 50% of your traffic will come from smartphones so make sure that you do the following:

A – Make your website "responsive" (your designer will know what this is)
B – It should load really fast!
C – Don't use any pop-ups or any invasive ads
D – Reduce heavy content
E – Make your checkout process short and sweet. Guest checkout should be an option as well.

Differentiating your brand requires a lot of time, effort, and even financial investment in your part. But if you're serious in building an ecommerce brand that will last, then you have to do as much differentiation strategies as possible. Differentiating means trying your best to become the best option for your customers. All of these boils down to serving the customers with the best of your ability. The more you differentiate, the more value you bring to your buyers who then turns into loyal customers.

In the next chapter, we'll talk about how to find your niche/idea and then we'll discuss the exact strategies to use for producing a product that people love and recommend to other people.

Chapter 2
How to Find Your Idea

Most beginners looking for their first niche or product idea start their research with products. They buy software tools and join online courses hoping they would get that "little nugget" of information that will lead them to their perfect first product. STOP. This doesn't work and this type of mindset will only lead you to failure.

Look for problems instead of products.

This is, quite frankly, what we are all doing in this business. We're just trying to solve someone's problem. We can tackle this in two ways.

Either solve a small problem that millions of people have, or solve a big problem that thousands of people have. So you can either focus on SCALE or MAGNITUDE. Truth be told, one is not better than the other.

You can sell lots of stuff and make millions or you can sell a decent amount of stuff and still make millions – it's just a matter of scale and the impact you are having in the market. Also, you don't necessarily have to choose one over the other to make money with ecommerce. The only key is to find a problem and solve it.

4 WAYS TO FIND PROFITABLE NICHE IDEAS

#1 - Self-Search/Products You're Already Using

I always start by looking within myself and finding problems that I am experiencing or something I experienced in the past.

Are there some products that you hope are available but aren't? Are you not satisfied with the products you are currently using? *Your facial wash? Your body bar? How about your shampoo?* Someone somewhere out there is complaining about something about a certain product. That someone could be you. You can turn this into an opportunity by creating a much better solution to the problem you are currently experiencing with the products you are using right now.

What are the problems that I am currently experiencing in my life?

What are the complaints that I have with the products that I am currently using?

Always listen to the type of language you are using on a daily basis.

For example, in the past few weeks, I've been having trouble with the following:

1 – Back Pain (oh God, every day is a struggle)
2 – Sleeping Consistency (zombie mode!)
3 – Having New Braces and Having a Hard Time Flossing
4 – Canker Sore (these little bastards hurt!)

These are all opportunities that can lead to a great product. These are all problems that I can solve for myself.

What are the products that are currently working for me but could be improved upon? What products do I currently use but aren't really working for me?

We're not trying to re-invent the wheel here and we're not exactly trying to go to Mars. All of our daily problems are also possibly something that other people are experiencing. Those are opportunities in disguise and they are problems we can solve for other people.

#2 - Amazon Market Gap

One of the best ways to find a niche idea that already has a proven market is via what I call "Amazon Market Gap Research"

It's basically the art of looking at well reviewed products on Amazon and then finding gaps in the market by reading the negative feedback that the customers left on Amazon.

I'm telling you right now, you DO NOT need to pay thousands of dollars for product research tools, and approaching research this way is going to be more beneficial for you long-term speaking.

In my book *Product Research 101*, I argued that product research tools should only be complementary tools instead of the main way to find products. And quite honestly, I think I changed a lot of minds with my approach.

So here's the skinny of how I do my Amazon research.

Step 1 - Look for products that already exist

By now, you should already have some kind of idea of what niche you want to be in. If not. I recommend that you go back to the first niche research idea. As an alternative, you can also look at the Amazon best-seller list. I recommend that you start with categories like:

A – Toys & Games
B – Beauty & Personal Care
C – Handmade Products

D – Home & Kitchen
E – Kitchen & Dining
F – Patio, Lawn & Garden
G – Sports & Outdoors
H – Tools & Home Improvement

I do not recommend starting with computers, electronics, camera, cell phones, or pretty much anything with some kind of electronic part to operate. (I would say small battery operated ones is an exception.) Most of these products are super expensive to source and could easily break which can cost you hundreds of thousands of dollars.

I'm not saying you shouldn't be in those niches EVER, I just recommend that you start outside those categories first so you can avoid losing money that you probably don't even have yet. I'm just being realistic here because I don't want you to quit this business in your first year.

Step 2 – Once you found a product, start reading ALL the negative reviews and make a list of their complaints.

For example, I found this product called LED Light Arm Band under the Reflective Gear sub-category.

[Image 2.1]

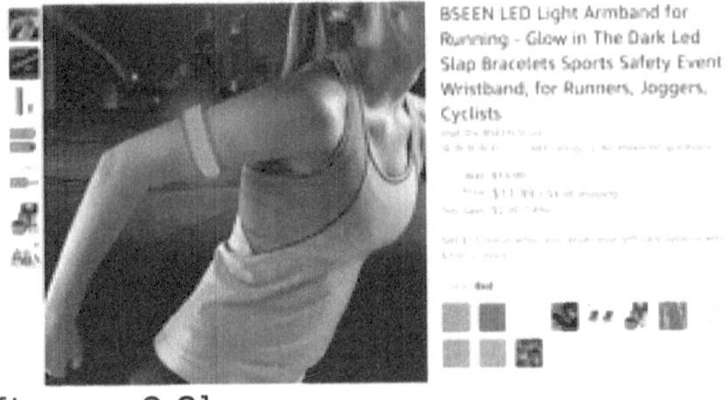

[Image 2.2]

This seems like an interesting product that solves a big problem for a lot of runners, which is getting seen and being visible in the dark.

So I dive deeper into the product and read some negative reviews.

By reading the 1-3 star reviews, I found out that the product issues are the following:

1 – The size is either too big for some women and too small for some men   [this seems to be number one concern]
2 – Hard to install and remove battery
3 – It's not that bright

After you found these issues, your job is to create a solution that will solve these problems for them. And that's basically how you create a better product that customers already want.

1 – Find a product that is already selling well
2 – Find the issues and concerns or the current market gaps
3 – Create a product that solves these issues

Just do this process over and over again and you'll have a variety of profitable niches to possibly be in.

A Note on **Value Skewing** (which we'll discuss a bit more on the latter part of this chapter):

I probably mention this technique in all of my books so I'm sorry if I have to repeat this over and over again (but it's that important). Once you found the things that you can improve upon, you have to choose the issues/concerns that your market values the most. You cannot possibly solve all of their problems but you can focus on the ones that are the most important to them. The more they complain about it, the more important it is to them that you solve that issue.

#3 - Google Trend Search

Using Google Trend is a good way to gauge the market's current demand or interest for a certain topic. *You obviously shouldn't limit your research with this tool as it only serves as an additional metric to evaluate the demand for the niche you are targeting.*

You can go to this link and log in using your Gmail account:

https://trends.google.com/trends/

When you use this tool, I recommend that you start with keywords directly related to the product that you want to sell.

Here are some examples:

1 – Product Based Keywords:

Fishing rods – this is a product name or a niche idea so I'll try to look at the 5-year data as well as the recent 12 months.

I like seeing graphs that looks more a bit like these:

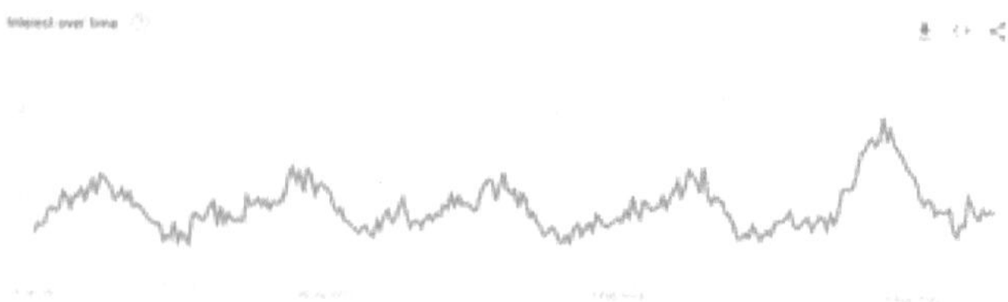

[Image 2.3]

[Image 2.4]

It doesn't go too up and down and it has a consistent number of searches.

Now that doesn't mean that it shouldn't have any peaks and lows, that's pretty normal…

For example, for the keyword "Electric toothbrush" [image 2.5], you will see in the 5 year graph below that there are some peaks and valleys especially during the last 3rd or 4th week of November.

But if you look at the graph as a whole, you will see that it's growing at a consistent 5% every year. Not exactly the hottest niche to be around but it's a consistent one nonetheless.

[Image 2.5]

2 – Problem/Solution Based Keywords:

I also like to look at keywords that mentions a problem or some kind of intention to find a solution.

For example, "Back pain massage"

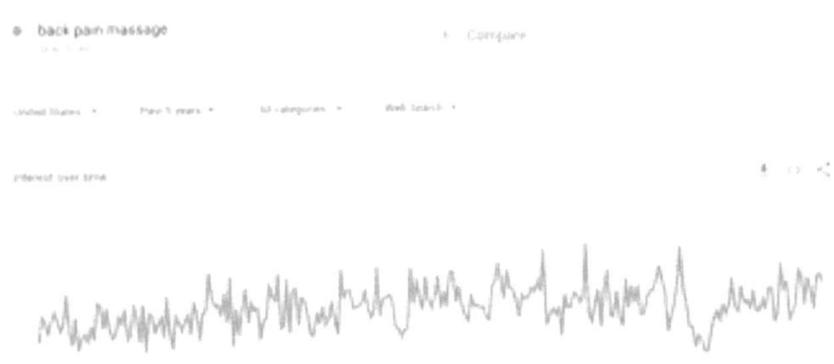

[Image 2.6]

So how do we evaluate these results?

Personally, I like to see trends that are either going up consistently for the last 5 years and/or something that isn't too cyclical or seasonal in nature.

I also like to target products that are timeless by nature. *For example, a back pain chair massage would probably still be useful in 2040. Humans have been experiencing back pain since the beginning of time and it's a problem that likely won't go away anytime soon. Fishing rods would always be in demand because humans will always feel the need to fish even just as a sport or a family outdoor activity. We can't help but do it because billions of our ancestors did it before us.*

The worst type of trends are fads like "fidget spinners." I would usually avoid going into markets that shows *wayyyyy* too much growth in such a limited amount of time (months, even days but not years). I would rather choose slow but consistent growth because there's higher likelihood that it will still be here to stay for a very long time. It's great to look at trends and ride that wave but be careful and use your best judgement because there's a good chance that you're only riding a fad.

#4 - Other People's Complaints

One of my favorite ways to find opportunities is by simply keeping my ears open for complaints. While other people shy away from hearing complaints, I'm always (at least in the back of my mind) open to hearing them.

We often hear people say things like:

This sucks…
I hate this…
I wish I could…
I wish there was…
Can this be any faster?
Why isn't there a…
I hate product X
I'd love to ______

All of these complaints are an opportunity to solve a problem. These are opportunities to create great products that are more likely to sell because they are solutions to common complaints.

This sucks… What sucks? Can you help this guy remove suckage?

I hate this… What do you hate? Can we make this better for you?

I wish I could… I wish there was a______ You wish you could what? Can you make a product that makes this wish possible?

Can this be any faster?... Can you make whatever this is, faster?

Why isn't there a... a what? Can we create this for you?

I hate product X... What do you hate about product x? Can we make a better one?

I'd love to have a _____ that does _________ .... What do you want and what does it do? I'd love to make this for you.

Always be on the lookout for these complaints and you'll be able to build a mind that is open to new opportunities. Have the mindset of a value creator and problem solver – that's how you come up with product ideas that sells.

How to Make Products Great Again

In a world full of instant, copy cats and shortcuts, I want you think about how you can be original. How can you solve the customers' problems and create value for other people?

This all revolves around the technique called **VALUE SKEWING**. It's about tailoring your products based on what the customers value. It's about skewing value out of things that your audience think are important.

Now, being original doesn't mean inventing a completely new product. It's more about figuring out what you can improve upon an existing product so you can serve the market better than everybody else.

If you followed my suggestions in chapter 1, then you'll know exactly which values you can skew to make a certain product better.

Here are the things to consider when you're value skewing:

#1 - Design

People love a better designed product. It makes them feel good using the product and it affects how we perceive a product's value. Look at what your competitors are doing and ask yourself, "Is there a way I can make this look and function better?"

Ask your supplier if they can create a better design for you. This again comes back to your research. What do the customers want and need? Give it to em' and watch the avalanche of sales come in.

#2 – Functions and Features

Is there anything it could do better?
Something it could do that it couldn't before?

Are there any new features you can add that your customers will appreciate?

In the world of motorcycles, ABS brakes used to be reserved only for big bikes and premium motorcycles. But today, ABS technology is slowly becoming a legal requirement to sell small or big bikes in some countries. It's because this feature, or this function of having ABS brakes has been proven to save lives and avoid accidents.

Look at your own product and find out what features it could have that will make your customers' lives easier and better. It doesn't even have to be some kind of new technology. For example, a simple change in *grippable* material for an electric shaver can alter the way the customer uses the product. Remember this: just one change in feature can elevate your product compared to the rest of your competition.

#3 - Price

If you're selling on Amazon, it wants your product to be as cheap as possible. Remember Amazon's motto, "the lowest price possible with the widest selection." Lower your price as much as possible.

If you're selling outside Amazon (on your own website), I still highly recommend that you go as low as your margins could allow. In the long-term, having an affordable and better offering is still the best business practice because it gives the customers' more value for their money.

#4 - Materials or Ingredients

In chapter 1, we talk about using different materials or ingredients that people love to see on the products they are buying.

For example, you can use ALL ORGANIC ingredients so you can add value to a market that demands that type of product. You can assure them by having a product that is 100% plant based, gluten free, vegan, dairy free, and soy free. Each one of these are one value being skewed in stack of another. So it all comes down to knowing your market. *What ingredients or materials do they want in their product? What ingredients do they want to avoid?* The more value you skew in their favor, the more likely they are to patronize your product.

Another part is adding ingredients that solves a specific problem.

Here are some examples:

Tranexamic Acid & Kojic Acid – Lightens Skin (a very good value stack for the Asian market who wants to have lighter skin)

Rhodiola – Reduces Stress (great for products that promises renewed energy and less stress)

Cranberry – Antioxidants, vitamins, and minerals (great for products that promises improvement in immunity and urinary health)

Look at the last few products you bought, especially the consumable ones (food, vitamins, skin care). They probably not only listed their ingredients but also mention the benefits of each one of them.

Applying the concept of Value Stacking is probably the best way to get new customers and retain them for the long-term. The key here is to add materials or ingredients that you can attach to a specific benefit.

The more value you stack in their favor, the more likely they are to convert as customers.

#5 – Customer Service

Ah, the forgotten art of good customer service. In today's business climate, a good customer service is now part of the product. I recommend investing in a full-time customer service representative either by email or by phone. It's a worthy investment and something that will serve your brand well.

#6 – Customer Experience

Another way to add value to your customers is by improving the buying experience.

Here are some best practices to follow:

1 – Make your website simple and easy navigate

2 – Make the colors easy to look at

3 – Give the benefits and features of the products

4 – Clear instructions on how to pay

5 – Offers fast shipping

6 – Easy to locate customer service, plus wider choices of communication (email, chat, and call)

7 – Shows product reviews below the product pages (SUPAH CRUCIAL!)

I recommend that you checkout ORGANIFISHOP since this is a really good example of a well-run ecommerce business. I have no affiliation with this company, I just really like the way they run their e-commerce business.

https://www.organifishop.com/

#7 - Main Benefits

Another value to stack is the main use or benefits of the product.

Can it solve a more painful (or at least a different) problem?

For example, the pillow was invented so that insects would not crawl on human's faces whenever we sleep. At some point, some smart dude pointed out the obvious and said "This sleeping on a piece of rock thing sucks." Then some smarter dude started using softer materials and here we are in the 21st century, spoiled in our cushy pillows. Thanks random smart dude or dudette!

The original recipe for Coca-Cola was actually used as cure for morphine addiction. There's a long history there but today we just drink it for our sugar addiction and it's legal too! Hooray, I guess.

My point is, try to find other uses for products that already exist. This is obviously a hard exercise to do but a good one nonetheless. It helps you transform your mind and it creates a shift in the way you think. By doing this exercise often, you start to become a value-creator instead of a copy-cat.

Chapter 3
Product Sourcing Made Simple

Your suppliers are the literal lifeblood of your product inventory. They're the ones who manufactures your product for you and they have control over whether you'll have something to sell or not.

In this chapter I want to show you the following:

a – Where and how to find the best suppliers for your product.
b - How to evaluate whether you should hire them or not.
c - How to make your first order so you can make the process as seamless as possible.

Where and How to Find Suppliers

#1 – Start Local or Focus on Product-Place Specialty

If it's possible and if it make sense financially speaking, then I highly recommend that you start local. And by local, I mean your city or state. If you're going to sell primarily in the U.S., that **Made in the U.S.A** badge will always have a big effect on how people perceive your product. If you think about it, where your product is made from is a "value stack" in itself. People still value the country, state, or place where the product is made from.

Start with Google Search

Pretty obvious advice but it works. Search for your product name + add the state, city, or county you live in. There may be some potential suppliers for your product in your local area. This makes the shipping cheaper and the communication easier for both parties.

Some example searches are:

Product Name + Private Label + State
Product Name + Private Label + County
Product Name + Private Label + Country
Product Name + Manufacturer + State
Product Name + Manufacturer + County
Product Name + Manufacturer + Country
Product Name + Supplier + State
Product Name + Supplier + County
Product Name + Supplier+ Country

Another thing to consider is the **Product-Place Specialty.**

Most of the time, a certain line of products are going to be manufactured in one concentrated place.

For example, if you want your own private labeled brand of whiskey, then you will most likely find most of the manufacturers in Tennessee.

In this case, you can start your search with keywords like:

Private label whiskey Tennessee
Whiskey distiller Tennessee

Obviously there are other states that you can also search for, but I recommend that you start with the place with the most concentrated manufacturer of whatever product you want to sell.

If you look at the data from stacker, https://stacker.com/stories/2571/top-industries-every-state, you'll see the top industries in every state and that would be a good indicator of potential product availability and affordability for whatever niche you are in.

In other cases, you will have to expand beyond your local state and go international. That doesn't mean that you have to choose China immediately. You still have to think about product-place specialty and see what country will produce the best product for you.

Remember, it's not just about the "Made in USA" badge of honor. Other countries also have their specialties too and that could also act as a value stack that your customers will value. *I.e. "Made in Italy" – cars, motorcycles, anything fashion related, "Made in the Philippines" – coconut products, delicacies, unusual desserts, "Made in Japan" – literally anything industrial that is of the highest quality and something that will still work until all of us die from climate change.* Stereotypes has some value after all.

#2 – Alibaba.com

This is the most common way to find Chinese suppliers and this is where most people get started, and that's for a good reason. There's millions of products here and most sellers can understand and speak decent English.
In addition, there's also Trade Assurance in Alibaba so you're safer in terms of not getting scammed and ghosted.

To search for a product, just simply type your product name on the search bar.

[Image 3.1]

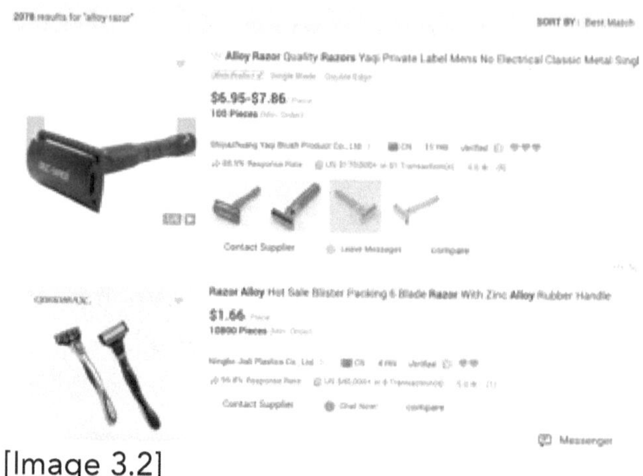

[Image 3.2]

There will always be a variety of style and colors to choose from so look for the design that you want for your own product. Also, don't hesitate to ask a supplier if they can change some things (either function or design) to fit your own vision of the product.

Here's a few advice if you choose to go this route:

a – Make sure that you're dealing directly with the manufacturer and not a broker so you can save money
b – Always read up on the company profile and check their website as well to see if they are legit
c – Always be polite in approaching their customer service
d – Be aware of their office hours if you want faster replies
e – Be patient because English isn't their first language

f – Don't ask stupid questions like "can I get a discount" on your first message.

Later in the chapter I'll show you how to evaluate your suppliers.

#3 – 1688.com

Here's another one of my new favorite website to use that is rarely discussed by those big time internet marketing gurus.
The process for research is pretty much the same as Alibaba and other platforms, so I'm just going to give you some of the best practices to follow if you use this platform.

A – Using 1688 requires an app called WeChat. It's like their WhatsApp over in China and it gives you direct communication with the manufacturer.

B – They mostly speak in Mandarin so use the WeChat app to translate whatever you want to ask them.

C – Use an extension called "Google Translate" on the Google Chrome store since the 1688 website is in Chinese.

D – The price that you will see on the product pages are already possibly the lowest they can give. Unlike Alibaba, the price on 1688 is mostly fixed because most (if not all) sellers here are wholesalers and direct manufacturers. Nonetheless, you can still negotiate with them especially if you're going to order more units.

E – The prices you see on 1688 are in RMB(CNY) so you need to have your currency converter handy. I just use the one provided by Google.

[Image 3.3]

You can also find free currency converter apps on the Apple or Android App Stores.

#4 – Make It Yourself

If you lack the capital and you have a lot of time, then why not learn to make the product yourself? This may not be possible for some people but
a lot of ecommerce businesses actually started this way.

If you make the product yourself, then it's going to be much cheaper to produce and ship since you have full control over the whole thing. In addition, you'll have higher profit margins and you'll make more money with a lot less capital investment.

Here are some ways to help you get started:

1 - Hire an Expert as a Consultant

If you really have no idea how to create the product and you're clueless about everything you need, then start with hiring an expert to teach you how to make it. Most experts will gladly work on a per hour basis as a consultant and you can just ask anything you want in that time.

2 - Hire an Expert to Create It with/or for You

Too lazy to learn everything by yourself? Then partner with an expert to create it with or for you. Most experts who can create products are notoriously bad marketers and entrepreneurs. Sure, they could be really good with the product creation part but most couldn't sell their way out of a paper bag even if their life depends on it. This is where you come in. You can be the Steve Jobs to their Steve Wozniak.

3 - Learn from Paid Online Courses or Free YouTube Videos

If you have almost zero budget, I recommend that you start with cheap online courses or free YouTube videos. You can pretty much learn everything on YouTube nowadays and there's just no excuse anymore not to get started.

EVALUATING YOUR SUPPLIERS

So how do you know which suppliers to work with? How do you make sure that you pick the right manufacturer for your awesome product?

That's where we use our 9-point criteria.

The more criteria we hit, the more likely we are to hire a specific supplier.

#1 – Direct Supplier/Manufacturer

Only work with direct suppliers or manufacturers who creates their own product. There's a lot of middle-man out there and they will naturally increase the price you pay per unit.

To avoid the middle-man, I always look at their company profile and even ask them directly if they are indeed the manufacturer and not just another company who will pass the work to other suppliers.

#2 – The price makes sense and you'll still make money selling the product

There's a lot of factors that will significantly affect your profit margin. Stuff like weight of the product, the packaging, and shipping options. This will obviously be different for every product, but as a general rule, I like to follow the 5X RULE. If you've read some of my books, then you probably already heard of this. In fact, I mention this in every single book I write and will continue to do so because it has serve me and thousands of my readers well.

The 5X RULE states that you should **sell your product for at least 5X the cost per unit to achieve breakeven point.**

That means if you want to be on the safe side, you should be able to sell a product on Amazon or your own website for at least 5x what it cost you to produce/source it.

For example, if your cost per unit is $5, then you should be able to see similar products on Amazon and other platforms that sells for at least $25.

The reason we want to follow the 5x rule as a general rule is because we won't necessarily know every single detail of our expenses until we're actually selling the product. There's just too many potential unexpected expenses that may creep up so we better bet on the safe side.

I recommend a tool called FBA Calculator if you want to go in-depth on expenses, Amazon fees, etc.

Here's the link for a free download:

https://junglescout.grsm.io/fbacalculator

#3 – You can actually afford the Minimum Order Quantity (MOQ)

Not all of us has an extra 5 million bucks just lying around the house, so we better make sure that we can actually afford to invest the necessary MOQ to produce the product.

Ask yourself, *what can I realistically afford to invest right now?*

#4 – Product and sample quality is up to par to your standards

Make sure that you order a sample and double check the quality of the product. Try its functions and see if it delivers on what it promises to do. If you're not thrilled about your own product, then chances are other people won't be as well.

#5 – Acceptable LEAD TIME [Manufacturing Lead Time]

Make sure that you agreed upon a specific time-frame of completion and shipping date. This is called lead-time. This is the amount of time they need to manufacture and package the product for it to be ready for shipping. If you're ordering from Alibaba or 1688, lead-time doesn't usually include the shipping time. This is something that you have to ask your suppliers since there are many types of lead-time and the definition may change depending on who you're talking to.

#6 – Clear Communication

The language barrier may play a part in this, but in general, I like to work with suppliers that replies fast and clearly. That means they should be able to answer my questions with clarity and I should be comfortable in asking them any questions related to my order. Not answering the questions and avoiding minute but important details is a big sign that you shouldn't work with a certain supplier.

#7 - Years in Business.

I usually only work with manufacturers who has been in the business for at least 5 years. There's going to be less risk of default and they already know the ins and out of manufacturing, shipping, and all that crazy stuff that us ecommerce business owners have to go through. A good manufacturer can act as a "quasi mentor" because of their experience. We just have to ask questions about things that we don't understand.

For example, when I was just getting started, I used to ask dozens of questions about the shipping process and they gladly responded to my questions in detail because I am a customer. This is how I was able to learn the shipping process fairly early in the game which I suspect has saved me thousands of dollars over the years.

#8 – Product Specs Change

Can they create new product mold? Can they change some aspects of the product to match your preferred specification, design, and features?
The more changes they can accommodate, the better.

#9 – You trust them (intuition)

You did your research, the numbers make sense, and the supplier check all the boxes. Now it's time to ask yourself: DO I TRUST THEM? Do you actually have a good feeling about this supplier. My intuition has played a big part in my e-commerce journey and the more I follow it, the more I seem to achieve success in my business.

MAKING YOUR FIRST ORDER

Now it's time to make your first order. If you did your research and you follow the criteria that I just showed you, then making you first order should be a breeze.

Step 1 - Negotiate the MOQ

First you have to ask yourself what you can realistically afford.

Be respectful in asking for any discounts and don't negotiate on the first message you sent. Try to build a relationship first and ask important questions related to the product so they'll know that you mean serious business.

Just know that if you are ordering from China and you're working with a direct supplier, then *they are most likely already providing you the lowest possible price.* Competition in China is fierce and these companies want to work with you in the long-term. They want to win your business and providing the lowest price possible is one of the keys for them to achieve that.

Step 2 - Make sure that the number works

Follow my 5x rule for this.

Step 3 - Get clear on the shipping

Make sure that you know who pays what. There's lots of type of shipping like: ex works, freight on board, and delivery duty paid.

Ex Works is when the seller is only responsible for making the product available to a specific designation (usually a port) and the buyer becomes responsible for everything else.

Freight on Board (FOB) is when the seller is responsible for shipping to the port (usually your country's port) and then you have to hire freight forwarders to ship it to your designated location.

There's many types of FOB so make sure to read up on it here:

https://corporatefinanceinstitute.com/resources/kno wledge/other/freight-on-board-fob/

Delivery Duty Paid is when the seller is responsible for everything till the product arrives at your preferred designation.

My advice: Research on the pros and cons of these options then slowly realize that Delivery Duty Paid is the best! Seriously though, if you're a beginner DDP is definitely the best option because you don't have to worry about anything else except making sure that the product sells.

Then there's the shipping method of either Air or Sea.

I can write a whole book about shipping (I actually did) so I'm just going to explain the skinny here:

1 - You have two main options if you're sourcing outside the U.S. It's either AIR OR SEA.

Air is going to be faster (usually 3-10 days) but it is more expensive.

Sea is going to be much cheaper (2x-3x cheaper than air) but it can take 30-45 days before it arrives to your preferred designation.

ADVICE: MIX THE TWO!

This allows you to learn both the shipping process for air and sea and it saves money as well since you're doing the other half via sea.

Note: Check out part 4 of this FBA series called FBA Product Sourcing Blueprint to get a whole step by step instruction on how to deal with shipping.

Chapter 4
How to Sell Your Physical Products

Start with Amazon FBA

I will tell you straight up that you should start with Amazon FBA because of these 2 things:

1 - Free Traffic

Amazon gets millions of visitors per day and a lot of them are already looking for the type of product you are selling. All you have to do is leverage Amazon's search engine and optimize your listing for the keywords you are targeting. With Amazon, you already have an existing audience that you know are ready to buy your product. If you did the value-skewing part of this training, then I have no doubt that you'll create a much better product compared to your competition.

2 – Paid Market Test

Even if you're not 100% sure that your product will sell like gangbusters, with Amazon, you'll also know if people are actually interested in purchasing your product. Even if you're spending money on Amazon Ads, you don't necessarily have to go broke to test things out. With Amazon, there's less risk of ordering inventories and not selling it because there's millions of potential customers who can see your listing.

Think of it as a paid market test. Whenever you're selling a new product, you're basically trying to test a hypothesis and you're trying to find out the truth. In this case, the hypothesis will always be "Is my product going to sell?"

You'll never really know until you test it and actually start selling your product online. The best place for you to do that is through Amazon FBA.

Signing-Up on Amazon

You can register for an account here:

https://sellercentral.amazon.com/

1 – You can start as an individual seller for free + fees

Or

2 – You can choose to become a professional seller for $39.99 a month

I recommend the second one since you're here to sell lots of stuff and not just flip items you found on eBay.

KEYS TO A SUCCESSFUL AMAZON BASED PRODUCT

#1 – Have a Damn Good Product

Just simply apply the lessons you learned in the past few chapters and I'll have no doubt that you'll create a superior product in comparison to your competition.

#2 – Keywords are Crucial

If you want to sell lots of stuff on Amazon, then you gotta target the right keywords that are highly related to your product. Most people think that long-tail keywords (3-4 terms, low searched) is the key to making money because they can easily ranked for it on Amazon. The truth is, it's all about the main/competitive keywords. It's all about the keywords that are getting thousands and thousands of searches. The good news is you don't need to have any of those paid keyword research tool to get started. You can simply use your common sense and look at what keywords your competition are using. Usually, you'll find these main keywords on the product title.

For example, if your product is a "car seat cover for dogs", then you can just type that term on Amazon and look at what the competition is doing.

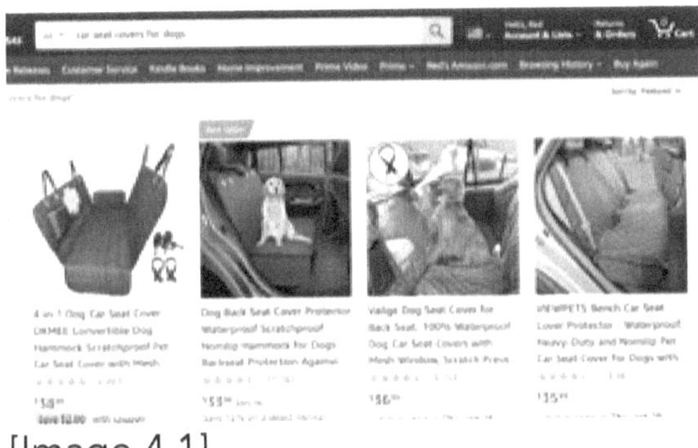

[Image 4.1]

Just by doing this research, I found out that my competitors are targeting the following keywords:

Waterproof
Scratchproof
Backseat Protection
Scratch Prevention
Cover Protector
Durable
Non-slip
Car Seat Cover for Dogs

You can then use these keywords for your title, Amazon keywords meta data, and other parts of your listing.

There's more strategies you can apply for keyword research but this is the most basic and easiest one to implement.

#3 – Creating a Highly Optimized Product Listing

Your listing acts as a 24/7 salesman for your product. He's your hype man. He's your #1 digital supporter and he will always only be as good the salesman that you made him to be.

You are responsible for putting your product in as good a light as possible and you can do that via your listing.

Here are the most important part of an Amazon listing:

A – Title. Always use your main keywords on your title but DO NOT overoptimized and just randomly mention the terms.

Here's a simple formula that works for me:

Brand Name + Primary Keywords + Main Features

1 – Start with your brand name.

2 – Choose the top 2-3 terms to put on your title as primary keywords. Make sure that they are relevant.

3 – Then add the most important features your customers need to know.

Example:

Ortho-Max | Biodegradable Bamboo Toothbrush | Eco Friendly, Soft Nylon Bristles, Organic Material, Smooth Handle, 100% Recyclable.

Quick tip: Make sure that you use a vertical bar to separate the 3 parts.

B – Bullet Points. Here's a simple formula for bullet points.

Line #1 - Feature + Benefits
I give them the biggest and most important feature that they are looking for and I explain how this affects them.

Line #2 - Feature + Benefits
I give them the 2nd biggest feature that they are looking for and I explain how this affects them.

Line #3 – Differentiate
I try to differentiate my product through a specific feature or benefit.

Line #4 - Twist the Knife + Solve the Problem
I give them a big problem and then I explain to them how my product solves this problem.

Line #5 - Guarantees
I give them some sort of guarantee that the product works or else they can send it back to me and get a 100% refund.

C – Images. Always use high quality images shot by professional photographers who specialize in physical products.

***

To get more info on keyword research and setting up your listing, I recommend the following resources:

https://www.wordstream.com/blog/ws/2018/10/23/amazon-keyword-research

https://blog.repricer.com/resources/complete-guide-amazon-keyword-research/

https://www.plytix.com/blog/amazon-keyword-research-for-brands

https://manychat.com/blog/amazon-listing-optimization/

https://www.repricerexpress.com/optimise-your-amazon-product-listings/

Surprise, surprise – my book! **Amazon Keyword Research 101** where I discussed how to find the best keywords without using any tool at all and how to create an effective product listing from start to finish.

***

How to Get Amazon Reviews

If you want more organic sales for your product, then you gotta have reviews that can act as your social proof. Customers love to buy products that other people are already using.

So how do you get consistent product reviews especially if you're just getting started

#1 - Lower your prices

In the beginning, you might want to consider lowering the prices to the point that you're only breaking even. This will get you more sales which means more people trying out your product. This is definitely a short-term sacrifice that will yield you great results in the future. Not everybody has the guts to do this because, quite honestly, it sucks not making a profit from your hard work. But if you choose to do this now, I have a feeling that you'll thank yourself 3-6 months down the road.

#2 - Product Inserts

This is the best way to convince your buyers to leave you an Amazon review. A simple message asking them to write a review on Amazon is all it takes to get tens or hundreds of reviews for your product. Now, never ever directly ask for a 5-star review (or a positive review for that matter) since this is against Amazon's terms.

What I like to do instead is put a subtle 5-star images below my product insert after the initial text asking for a feedback.

Here's an example:

[Image 4.2]

Asking them to contact customer service if there's any issue is also one of the best ways to avoid getting a negative review.

***

Warning: Don't pay for any reviews as it is against Amazon's terms and you'll risk your selling account getting banned forever.

SELLING ON YOUR OWN WEBSITE

The next step on your progression it to start selling on your own website. So when do you start doing it? When does it make sense to start creating your own mark outside Amazon?

I'd say when these 2 things start happening:

#1 – When you start getting at least 10 sales per day on Amazon

This means your product is a proven hit. You may not be making millions yet but you know that this product has the potential to be a 7-figure product line. You know that this is a proven market because you're getting consistent sales even without spending money on ads.

#2 – When you can already afford to pay for advertisements

I recommend starting with at least $3,000 in ad budget if you're going to advertise outside Amazon.

Don't worry because you don't necessarily have to spend all of it in just one week. In the beginning, the goal is to test things out and breakeven. You can get started with Facebook Ads and then expand to other platforms if you want to scale even more.

What Platform Should You Use?

I recommend that you start with Shopify.

It's easy to use and its monthly membership is pretty affordable.

Prices may differ depending on where you live, but here's the current membership options available in North America.

	Basic Shopify	Shopify	Advanced Shopify
	All the basics for starting a new business	Everything you need for a growing business	Advanced features for scaling your business
Monthly price	USD $29/mo	USD $79/mo	USD $299/mo
SHOPIFY PAYMENTS			
Fraud analysis	✓	✓	✓
Online credit card rates	2.9% + 30¢	2.6% + 30¢	2.4% + 30¢
In-person credit card rates	2.7% + 0¢	2.5% + 0¢	2.4% + 0¢
Additional fees using all payment providers other than Shopify Payments	2.0%	1.0%	0.5%

[Image 4.3]

Keys to a Successful Shopify Store for Beginners

#1 - A Great Product

I hope that you noticed by now that, in my opinion, this is the number 1 thing that all ecommerce business owners should focus on. A great product allows you to sell and even overhype the product as much as you can because you know that it delivers "the goods."

It's easy to be confident in what you are selling when you know that your product works. So always focus on this one first before you even think about any marketing strategies. **A great product IS, bar none the best marketing strategy**. Highlight that, tattoo it in your wrist, I don't care what you do – just don't forget that it's the #1 thing that you should remember from this book.

#2 - Clean Looking Store Theme

Go for more neutral colors and don't overdesign it. I recommend using a combination of 2 colors in addition to white. Go for simple instead of complicated and "award winning" designs. F award winning designs. What does that even mean? Does that mean it makes more money? Or does it mean that a bunch of design nerds who knows nothing about marketing just gathered one evening and voted who has the best designed website… nah, *forgetabouthatcrap.*

Just focus on featuring the product and making sure that you mention its benefits and features. Your website should also be easy to navigate and it shouldn't be *laggy.* One of the most annoying thing that you can experience as a buyer is a slow website. So make sure that you make your site's loading speed is as fast as possible. Just search for "page load optimizer or page speed optimizer" on Shopify's app store and install the highest rated one.

Check out these 2 websites as a great example:

Supply.co – Single Edge Razors
Organifishop.com – Green Juices and Other Health Products

#3 – Paid Advertisements, Then Content Marketing

You don't want to rely on ads in the long term but it is a good way to start introducing your product to the market.

Since you're selling outside Amazon, you have to come up with your own traffic and the fastest way to do that is through paid ads. Once you have ads that are consistently making money every day, then you can start investing some of that profits to your content marketing (which is a long-term play for your business since it's not going to immediately make you any sales in the beginning).

Facebook Ads

FB is probably the easiest ad platform to learn and there's already thousands of free or paid courses available to study. Heck, even just FB's free guide can get you to $1,000 ad spend per day without any problem. You don't have to spend $5,000 with an fb ads guru to learn how to start and scale your ads. Facebook has their own learning platform and you should start with that.

Check out some of these resources to help you get started:

https://www.facebook.com/business/learn

https://www.facebook.com/business/ads-guide

https://neilpatel.com/blog/deep-dive-facebook-advertising/

So what are the keys to making Facebook Ad work for you?

A - Right Targeting

Who are you selling to. You can't say "everyone" because everyone does not exist. *Where do they live? What's the age range? What is their profession? Are they men or women? What things to they like to follow on Facebook? What are their political leanings (left? right?).* All these things add up to an avatar of what a potential buyer would be like. For example, a liberal is more likely to buy anything cat related than a conservative one. Obviously, political affiliations can only get you so much insights and it isn't always applicable without deeper research.

The point is to consider the avatar you are selling to and try to find out as many commonalities about them as possible.

B - Right Images/Videos

I recommend at least an iPhone quality shot or professional photographs that doesn't look like you got it from a stock photo website. Do not use any stock photos because they're eerily perfect and you'll find that your competition might be using them as well.

HOT TIP: Always use PEOPLE in your ad images. They convert better with pretty much any product.

For videos, short previews of the products converts the best. You don't have to start with those million-dollar infomercials. Start with the camera on your phone, shoot different angles of your product + a demo of someone using the product.

C - Longer Testing + One Variable at a Time

Most people spend $500 in 2 days and quit when they didn't get 100% ROI. This is stupid. Spend $10 per day and run 3 different ads with the same everything except for the AD creative/image itself. For example, if I'm selling a single edge razor, I would create 3 ads with the same ad angle, same ad body copy, same targeting and then use 3 different images. I will only test one variable at a time so I'll know which exactly is the factor that affects my ad results the most.

Test at least 3 ads in the beginning and find out the winner within 5-7 days. DO NOT change anything for the first 7 days. DO NOT even touch your ads. Your goal is to let the machine do the work and find out what is the best ad for your product. After the first 7 days, you'll have a clear winner which is obviously the one with the best ROI.

Most of the time, you'll test 3 ads, 2 will probably be at negative ROI and the other one will be at least BREAKEVEN. In this case, breakeven was the winner. Keep running the breakeven ad for another 7 days and let it learn on its own. Most likely, this ad will turn into a winner if you just let it run for an extended amount of time. An ad needs time to learn who the type of person it should target before it starts producing better results. If you're not patient and you're not willing to test, then you won't be able to make Facebook Ads (or any ads for that matter) work for you.

Instagram Marketing

Start with Influencer Marketing

Influencer Marketing is about finding people on social media platforms and then working together to promote your product for you.

I recommend using Buzzsumo's tool for finding influencers on your niche.

https://buzzsumo.com/find-influencers/

Look for micro influencers. 10,000 - 30,000 followers is the best for higher conversion. They are cheaper to work with, and converts higher especially if you pick active ones. Make sure that they're posting at least 2-

3 times per week plus don't forget to look at their profile and see if they are communicating with their followers. If it's just a bunch of semi-nude photos with thirsty men commenting about how hot the influencer is, then just RUN AWAY – fast!

What you want is an influencer who can represent your product in a good light. You want someone who you can work with long-term and build a win-win relationship with.

Here's the price range for influencer at the moment of writing this:

1. An influencer with 10,000 followers could charge $100 per post

2. An influencer with 100,000 followers could charge $1000 per post

3. An influencer with 1,000,000 followers could charge $10,000 per post

https://www.webfx.com/influencer-marketing-pricing.html#instagram-influencer-pricing

Content Marketing

This is more of a long term approach so you shouldn't expect to make thousands of sales from your content marketing efforts – at least not in the first few months.

With content marketing, I recommend that you **don't** start with just 1 platform. I recommend that you start with **1 MEDIUM** instead. Mediums are the way you deliver your content: Is it written? Is it audio? Or is it videos? I recommend that you go heavy on VIDEOS + some photos every now and then.

With videos, you can share them on each and every single one of your platform. You can share them through Facebook, Instagram, YouTube and even your own blog and just add a few text explaining what the video is all about.

What type of video content should you create?

Targeted Topics - look for mini problems that they want to solve along the way. Shoot some instructional videos on how to solve a specific problem by using your product.

Case Studies – you can also show some case studies of customers whose life has been improved because of your product.

Testimonials (Before and After) – people love to see other people getting good results because they imagine that it would happen to them as well. Show some testimonials, preferably with some kind of before and after visuals so they can imagine themselves using your product.

Video is BIG everywhere and you can grow your business faster if you take advantage of it. It's the best way to dominate your market in 2021, 2022 and beyond.

Side Note: If there's a demand (which I can see on the reviews of this book, I'll probably write a marketing guide focusing on this aspect alone).

Additional Resource:

Finding cheap traffic can be hard nowadays. Every big ad platform now are a bit of a pain in the butt to work with. As I was editing this chapter, I discovered an article by Charles Ngo where he talks about finding underpriced sources of traffic and looking for opportunities in the market so you can grow your business.

Check it out here:
https://charlesngo.com/underpricedtraffic/

It doesn't matter whether you're reading it in 2021, 2022 or 2030. The main point is to always be on the lookout for undervalued opportunities and start taking advantage of them as soon as possible.

Chapter 5
How to Scale Your Ecommerce Brand

Taking your business to the next level will require some input that most people just ignore. The truth is, some ecommerce sellers are already satisfied in making $60-100k per year (basically, a full-time income) - and if that's you, then kudos to you and you should enjoy the fruit of your labor. Do what's important to you and do whatever makes you happy. Sometimes, the money we make beyond what we need is just a distraction for living a life that will truly make us fulfilled.

But if you want to expand beyond that, then it will take some more time investment and additional work. The good news is these additional work are doable even for people who doesn't have a huge budget or cashflow yet.

Here are 5 Strategies to Expand to 7-Figures Per Year

#1 - Sell Other Products

When other ecommerce business owners ask me how they can improve their sales and overall, their brand's identity - all I say to them are these 3 words.

SELL OTHER PRODUCTS.

If you think about it, most of the billion dollar brands out there sell multiple products at the same time. Different products solve different needs. So all you have to do is find products that are similar or complementary to what you're already selling.

For example, if you sell razors, then the natural complementary products for that are blades, shaving cream, post shave oil, face wash, and moisturizer. These are the complementary products that matches your original one. If you're selling a quality razor, then they shouldn't need to buy it every week. That means you won't have anything to sell to the customer who already bought your razor if you don't have any of those complementary ones. In addition, remember that it's 5x easier to sell to a current customer than with a new one. In terms of cost per customer acquisition, you won't really need to spend that much to convert your current customers on new product offerings.

Want to expand to 7-figures? Then start selling other products that also adds value to your customers' lives.

#2 - Cart Abandonment

This will depend on what platform you're using so I couldn't give you a specific instruction on how to do this.

I do recommend that you install some kind of automation that emails customers whenever they abandon their cart. Majority of people who click **add to cart** will actually won't proceed to paying the item. This means you're losing hundreds of sales that you could've easily gotten already.

I recommend that you offer a discount or *special offer* to anyone who abandons their cart.

For example, Organifishop.com sends a 3-day email sequence to anyone who abandons their cart and they offer an additional 10% discount to anyone who will continue with the checkout process.

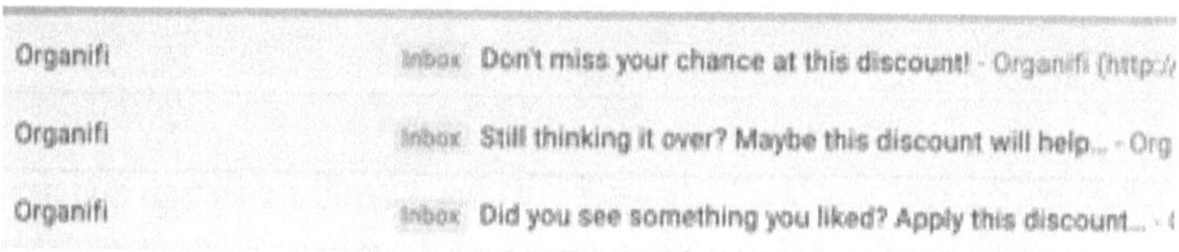

Organifi   Inbox   Don't miss your chance at this discount! - Organifi (http://

Organifi   Inbox   Still thinking it over? Maybe this discount will help... - Org

Organifi   Inbox   Did you see something you liked? Apply this discount... - (

[Image 5.1]

This is a great way to get customers who are on the cusp of purchasing your product but couldn't quite pull the trigger because of some lingering doubt in their minds.

The job of the offer is to make the buying decision easier for them.

To make the offer even better, I recommend that you also put a time-bounded discount link that will expire in 3 days. This makes them act faster and it encourages your customers to make a decision now.

#3 - Raise Your AOV

AOV or your average order value is the total amount you make on average per customer order.

To calculate your company's **average order value**, simply divide your total revenue by the number of **orders**. For example, let's say that in the month of September, your web store's sales was $31,000 and you had a total of 1,000 **orders**. $31,000 divided by 1,000 = $31, so September's monthly **AOV** was $31.

Here's a few things you can do to increase your AOV:

Offer a free shipping threshold... Offer free shipping to anyone who will have an average order value of $75 or more. I recommend offering free shipping to anyone who orders double of what your current AOV is.

Offer other products... The more products for them to add to cart, the higher your AOV could be.

Offer time sensitive deals... Every 4 weeks or so, you can offer some kind of time-sensitive deals for your complementary products.

Upsells... Make sure that you offer different product specifications like colors, specs, and sizes so you can upsell a more expensive version of your products.

Apple is the master of doing this so you should take a look at how they make their offers and upsells.

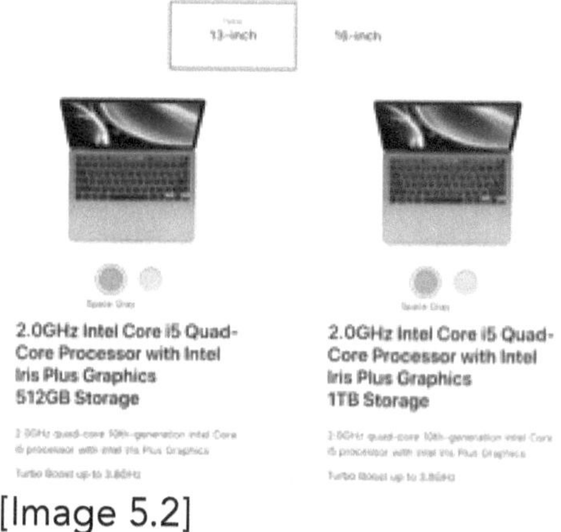

[Image 5.2]

#4 - Focus on Your Email List

Your email list is your number 1 marketing asset. I would rather have 100,000 people on my list than 2,000,000 Instagram followers. With email, I can reach them directly and I can communicate better due to the nature of how we read emails.

I recommend that you send your customers weekly emails talking about new products, special offers, customer testimonials, a new video that you made and pretty much anything that adds value to your customer.

Here are some resources to check out when it comes to ecommerce email marketing:

https://sleeknote.com/blog/e-commerce-email-marketing

https://www.sendinblue.com/blog/ecommerce-email-strategy/

https://neilpatel.com/blog/bootstrap-e-commerce-sales/

#5 - Scale Through Ads

You should never rely on ads alone but that doesn't mean you shouldn't run them. Ads are still a great source of consistent sales because more people will be seeing your product listing on a consistent basis.

THE ROI WASH APPROACH

Most people think that they have to have hundreds of thousands of dollars already to get started with online ads. Not really, not if your smart enough to implement what I call the ROI WASH APPROACH.

Here's what usually happens when other people run ads online.

#1 – They have some sort of fixed advertising budget.

#2 – They start running ads and they go "all in" – "I'm gonna run this ad till I lose x amount of money [the fixed budget]"

#3 – They lose it all or they lose 25%-50% and they, pardon my French, b*tch about ads being a scam

Here's what you should do instead:

THE ROI WASH APPROACH

THE NUMBERS

Example:

Start with $500, make $400 back... that's a loss.

Re-invest $400 back into ads, this time using better data that you gathered from your initial "loss." Re-adjust you ad strategy and create a better ad or better targeting.

From that $400, you'll probably make $700 back because you now have better and more accurate data for your ads. Even if you're still at the breakeven point or negative ROI, you're now in a better position to run your ads because of you have a more accurate set of data.

Keep re-investing that $700 back…

Let's say that you made $1,000 ($300 profit from that initial $700). Don't go party around and don't buy any fancy stuff. Just re-invest that $1,000 again to the business and just keep growing your treasure chest.

The key is to re-invest your ROI over and over again. It's like washing your ROI, thus it's called the "ROI WASH" method.

THE APPROACH

#1 – Start running small ads just like what I taught you in the FB ads part in chapter 4.

#2 – You'll likely lose 20%-30% of your ad budget but you will still make sales. It's likely that you'll also get to breakeven. The goal in the beginning is to gather data so you can re-adjust your targeting/ad message later.

#3 – Even if you lose 20%-30%, you probably were still able to make some sales. **START RE-INVESTING YOUR SALES INTO YOUR ADS.**

Okay, this is crucial so read this again.

START RE-INVESTING YOUR SALES INTO YOUR ADS. This is how the pros do it. They don't quit when they get negative ROI. They just re-adjust and find what works and they start re-investing their sales into their ads. By doing this, you'll be able to increase that ad budget again and keep testing.

#4 – After you re-adjust your strategy, you'll probably start making positive ROI. Usually, for e-commerce, you'll see that gurus are bragging about 100%-500% ROI. That's crazy and that's not scalable. You should aim for 10%-20% instead since it's a bit more realistic.

#5 – Once you start making that positive ROI, just re-invest that profit back again to the ads. This is how you grow an ad budget and this is how you make money long-term.

Just keep washing that ROI and keep on improving your ads. Eventually, you'll get higher returns and you'll have a sustainable business that gets consistent profits day-in and day-out.

BONUS - Test Those Trinkets

There will always be little things that will help you grow your ecommerce business. Most of the time, you'll have some kind of app that do whatever those little things are. For example, "Referral Candy" allows your customer to share your products and they'll get to have discounts that they can use on your store. It's a win-win. Another one is called "Subscription by Recharge" which allows you to sell products on a subscription basis. There's all kind of apps with different functions and it's your job as an ecommerce business owner to test things out and see if they will work for your own store.

Check out the following link to read more about these apps that you can test for your own store.

https://www.referralcandy.com/blog/best-shopify-apps/

https://www.optimonk.com/shopify-app-store-best-shopify-apps-drive-sales/

Note: Not all of them will have a major impact on your business but it won't hurt to test things out so you'll find out what works for your own brand.

Conclusion

The right action will give you the awesome results you are aiming for. But most people get lost in the process and gets overwhelmed by what they have to do. So here are some quick actionable advice I want to give you before I let you off the hook (*or before you read another one of my books – wink-wink)...*

1 - Decide if this business is for you. By now you already have an idea of how much time, effort and money it takes to start and grow an ecommerce business. There's no shame in realizing that this type of business isn't for you. In fact, I would assume that at least half the people reading this isn't going to do anything about the information they just learned. Another 50% will probably dabble into it and start looking for products, and then 1-2% will actually proceed into selling it on Amazon or on their own websites. If you want to be in that top 1%-2% - then you have to fully commit to it.

2 - Start looking for problems, then start researching product ideas. Focus your attention in trying to solve real-world problems. Start with your own problems and then expand to the people around you. Always be on the lookout for problems that you can solve since these issues may turn into a profitable product idea.

3 - Create a brand identity that makes you excited. Try to create a brand identity that makes you want to work on your business. If your personality is quirky and bubbly, then you may want to incorporate that to your own brand. It's always nice to see founders bring some much needed energy to an ecommerce brand and not just focus on how much money they will make.

4 - Choose a selling platform. You can either start with Amazon or your own website. I always recommend that people start with Amazon because of the free traffic, but if you already have some marketing and advertising skills – then you can go straight to having your own store since you'll have more control over your own brand.

5 - Choose one "customer getting" method. Lastly, you should focus on just one customer acquisition method especially in the beginning. This allows you to get better results [aka more profits], that you can then leverage and re-invest on other parts of your business like customer service, product improvement, faster shipping, and other advertising platforms. Hopefully, I was able to give you some valuable information that you can use in your journey to starting and growing your own brand.

I wish you all the best in this amazing journey,

Red

OTHER FBA BOOKS

AMAZON FBA Step by Step (by Red Mikhail) – to help you get started with Amazon FBA (the basics)

FBA Product Research 101 – an in depth guide to product research

Amazon Keyword Research 101 – an in depth guide to Amazon keyword research

FBA Product Sourcing Blueprint – a step by step blueprint on sourcing products and shipping it to Amazon/your preferred destination

Amazon FBA Sales Boost – 33 little tricks to triple your Amazon sales

These are also available as audiobooks.

You can find the whole series here:

https://www.amazon.com/gp/product/B086QZCJQQ

Review Request

As you might already know, reviews are the lifeblood of every author out there. If you found some value in this one, allow me to humbly ask for a review on Amazon as it does help in spreading my message.

Thank you so much and good luck on building your ecommerce brand.